WHY THE RABBI PLAYED CLARINET IN THE SAUNA

BY DINA SHTULL

ILLUSTRATED BY LORETTA BRADFIELD

WHY THE RABBI PLAYED CLARINET IN THE SAUNA

BY DINA SHTULL

ILLUSTRATED BY LORETTA BRADFIELD

Rabbi Jacob Shtull (1925–2002)
Zichrono Livracha. His memory is a blessing.

For his great-grandchildren, Ada, Gabriel, Nitzan, and
those yet to come.
May they be inspired by his zest for life.

And for the great-grandchildren of the world.
May they be inspired to ask about their great-
grandparents and rejoice in their legacy.

Introduction

This book is about my father. My father had a number of names. At work, he was Rabbi Jacob Shtull, Rabbi Shtull, or sometimes just Rabbi. At home, he was Dad, or *Abba* in Hebrew. His wife, Rita, also called him *Abba*, the name sticking from the days she modeled the name for her children. The grandchildren called him *Saba*, Hebrew for grandfather. My father had yet another name—*Jack*, the name he was called as a child. In this book, I refer to my father as *Jack*. I use this name because it reminds me that I know about his childhood through stories. It helps me appreciate the value of telling stories about the people we love.

Judaism teaches that the most important "crown," or trait of public leadership, is having a good name (*Ethics of the Fathers*, 4:17). My father wore the crown of a good name. When I have the opportunity to introduce myself as Rabbi Shtull's daughter, invariably the comments are full of respect: "He was a nice man." "He was a good-hearted person." "I liked your dad."

With deep gratitude, I receive and pass along my father's legacy: Make the most of your moments. And don't forget to laugh along the way.

Dina Shtull

SOME WORDS THAT MAY BE NEW TO YOU

Brit Milah: Hebrew term for the ceremony that welcomes a baby boy into the Jewish religion.

Bat Mitzvah: Hebrew term for a Jewish girl who has arrived at the age of responsibility. It also refers to the ceremony celebrating this event.

Hebrew: Hebrew is one of two official languages of the State of Israel; the other is Arabic.

Rabbi: This is the title given to a Jewish religious leader and teacher. Other religions use different titles for their religious leaders, such as priest or imam.

Sauna: A sauna is a very hot room. People like to relax in a sauna.

Shabbat: Shabbat is the Hebrew word for the Sabbath. In Judaism, Shabbat is a day of rest and a special day to be with family and friends. The idea for the Sabbath comes from the Bible. The Bible says that God created the heavens and the earth for six days. On the seventh day, God rested and was refreshed (Exodus 31:17). In Judaism, the Sabbath begins at sundown on Friday and ends at nightfall on Saturday, when three stars appear in the sky. In other religions, the Sabbath may fall on other days and have other meanings.

Synagogue/shul: Jews gather in a synagogue for prayer, study, community service, and celebrations in much the same way that Christians gather in a church or Muslims gather in a mosque. A synagogue can also be called a *temple.* In the Yiddish language, a synagogue is called a *shul* [shool].

Yiddish: Yiddish is a language spoken by many European Jews and their descendants.

On November 18, 1925, a new baby boy was born in Montreal, Canada. His parents named him Jack and introduced him to his three older brothers, Joe, Phil, and Alex. Jack was a friendly baby. Even before he knew any words, he babbled all day long. When he learned to talk, he chattered incessantly. He always had a story to tell. When he learned to read, he spent hours in the library, stocking up on stories. Jack loved stories, whether he was reading them, telling them, or listening to them.

But Jack also loved to play. He played many sports, but like most children, he had his favorites.

He loved skiing during the winter

and swimming during the summer.

When Jack was a boy, he dreamed of becoming a rabbi. He told himself stories about what he would do as a rabbi.

Jack would share stories about the Jewish people and learn the stories told by people from other religions. Through stories Jack would teach people to be kind to one another.

Jack would help people celebrate when they were happy and comfort people when they were sad.

When Jack grew up, he began studying to become a rabbi. He studied for five years. He loved being a student, but sometimes he felt lonely. He wanted a good friend. Where could he meet that special person?

One evening Jack went to a dance. There he met Rita. They became wonderful friends. Jack and Rita decided to get married so that they could always be together. They never forgot that they met while dancing. For the rest of their lives, they always loved to dance together.

After working for a few years as a rabbi, the time came for Jack to look for a new job. By then, Jack and Rita had two small children, and Rita was pregnant with their third child. While he was away, Rita and the children went to visit her parents in New York City. The children loved visiting their grandparents. They loved hearing their stories about when they were little.

Finally, Jack called Rita with good news. He had a job!

Rita also had good news for Jack. They had a new baby girl! Jack was very happy, but he was also worried. He knew the apartment in New York was very small. Where would the baby sleep? Rita told Jack not to worry.

The baby slept in a drawer!

Jack laughed loudly. What a good story he would have to tell!

Jack's last name was *Shtull*. Rabbis are called by their last name, so Jack was called *Rabbi Shtull*. Then, people started calling the synagogue where Jack worked *Shtull's Shul*. Jack walked to and from Shtull's Shul every Shabbat. Jack walked when it was hot, and he walked when it was cold. He walked when it rained. He walked when it snowed. Jack walked in the morning, and he walked at night. His closet was full of gloves, scarves, hats, boots, umbrellas, and coats and jackets. That way he could walk in every season, no matter what the weather.

But Rita was concerned when Jack walked at night. She wanted him to be safe. How could Jack walk safely at night? He finally thought of a solution.

Jack wore a bright orange reflective vest. Now, passing cars could see him.

What Jack liked most about being a rabbi was teaching. He loved teaching the oldest ladies. And they loved him. They loved telling him stories about their children and grandchildren, and he loved to listen. This made the ladies love him even more.

Once, one of the ladies got sick. Her name was Henrietta. Henrietta lived alone. She did not have a family. Who would take care of her?

Jack would take care of her! His wife, Rita, would help.

Jack and Rita told Henrietta to call their house every morning. If Henrietta did not call, Jack and Rita knew Henrietta did not feel well. One morning, Henrietta did not call. What could Jack and Rita do?

They visited Henrietta and helped her get better.

Jack helped many people feel better when they were sick. But he also helped people in other ways.

Once, he helped a postman receive an award.

At the end of every day, Jack had to move his car to the other side of the street. But there were always so many cars, it was sometimes hard to find a new parking spot. One day, Jack noticed an empty spot. How could he save the parking spot while he moved his car?

Jack asked a passing postman if he would stand in the empty spot. The postman agreed. Later, Jack wrote a letter to the post office about the story of the postman and his kind deed. The post office gave the postman an award for his kindness.

Another person Jack helped was a man who sold him a suit. The salesman told Jack his story about how his relatives lived far away in Israel. The salesman was sad, because he did not see his relatives very often. But Jack and his family were going to Israel for a summer vacation. Jack would gladly visit the salesman's family. The salesman was so happy! He gave Jack many gifts to bring with him.

In Israel, Jack and his family visited the salesman's relatives. They gave them the gifts and told them stories about the salesman.

Jack loved visiting with people in Israel. He spent time with cousins and with friends from other religions. He also explored Israel's narrow streets and busy markets. Jack loved to speak Hebrew. He especially liked to bargain in Hebrew.

Jack liked being active. Even as an adult, he liked to run and play. He also liked doing household chores. He cleared the leaves from the gutters and planted and weeded a garden. He washed and fixed his own car. Jack was not lazy.

Once, Jack was supposed to be at a meeting with many rabbis from different cities. A meeting with rabbis meant lots of talking and storytelling, which Jack liked, but it also meant lots of sitting still, which Jack didn't like.

Soon, some of the rabbis noticed that Jack wasn't there. No matter where the rabbis looked, they could not find Jack. Where could he be?

Jack was skating on a frozen pond!

Jack loved skating so much that he even built a skating rink for his children in the backyard.

When Jack wasn't playing sports, telling stories, or helping people, he was learning to play the clarinet. Jack loved the clarinet so much that he practiced every day. But sometimes, his playing was just too loud for Rita.

Where could Jack practice?

Jack found a tiny space in the corner of the basement. The tiny space was in a little room called a sauna. Most people use a sauna as a place to relax, but not Jack and Rita. They didn't fill it with heat. They filled it with boxes. The boxes were filled with clothes they no longer wore and dishes they no longer used. Jack found just enough space to squeeze a chair and a music stand into that room. He was happy, and so was Rita!

Jack loved musical instruments. He bought recorders, violins, saxophones, flutes, and clarinets from families who no longer used them. The instruments all had their own stories about who played them and what music they had played. What could Jack do with all these instruments?

He gave them to his children and grandchildren.

Jack played his clarinet in a band. He joked that he sat in the back so the audience could not hear him.

a hAAAA ha Ha! HA HA!

Jack loved to laugh. His favorite joke was the one he happened to be telling. He laughed the loudest at his own jokes.

a hAAAA ha Ha! HA HA!

Jack laughed when he told the story about his family's business in Montreal. His family bought eggs from a farm and sold them to stores. They called the business "The Egg Factory." Why did Jack think this was so funny?

He knew that eggs are not made in factories.

The Egg Factory was in an old building. That building had not always been used to store eggs. Once, it had been a synagogue. In the back of the building, there was a pile of old stained-glass windows. The windows were made from small pieces of colored glass arranged in the shape of a six-pointed star. They were from the synagogue! What could the family do with the windows?

The family chose the most beautiful windows and brought them to Shtull's Shul, where they are to this day.

In the shul, there is a photograph of Jack. This is the picture.

Pictures help us remember stories. When people look at Jack's picture, they remember Jack's stories. They remember his good life. Now you too know Jack's stories. And you know why the rabbi played clarinet in the sauna.

More Pictures of Jack

Jack skiing with friends, Montreal, Canada, circa 1945

Jack and Rita, Brooklyn, New York, 1951

Jack with student, Camp CRUSY, Chelsea, Michigan, 1963

Jack serving as rabbi, Brit Milah, 1978

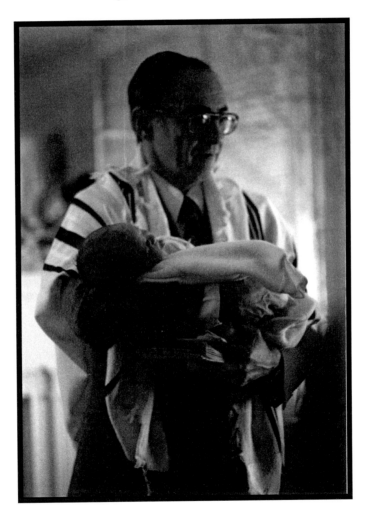

Dina Shtull and her father (Jack), Cleveland, Ohio, 1981

Jack dancing with Rita, granddaughter's Bat Mitzvah, 1998

Jack, Rita, and their four children (from left to right: Ora, Dina, Kiva, Simcha), in front of ark with stained-glass windows, Congregation Shaarey Tikvah, Cleveland, Ohio, 1999

Jack playing clarinet, Cleveland, Ohio, 2000

Author's Note

How do children share the life story of a parent? Do we rely on random occasions that may remind us to share a story? Do we expect that our stories, when we are moved to tell them, will be interesting to others? Will a photo book, pulled out at the right moment, receive undivided attention? Will a biography be read by anyone besides the immediate family? In thinking about these options, I decided to write a book for children, a book that parents would enjoy reading to their children, or a book that children could enjoy reading on their own. I hoped that a children's book might be easier to read—and therefore, more likely to be shared. The book would be my way of passing along my father's legacy. It would allow me to share life lessons that have passed the test of time.

Many people helped me in the process of writing this book. I am truly grateful to them. To my illustrator, Loretta Bradfield, for adding impact. To Janice Lieberman, school librarian, for wisdom and expertise, and for welcoming a test reading to the students at the Hebrew Day School of Ann Arbor. To the students; their insights were beyond their years. To Laurie Leflein, for deep appreciation of legacies. To my mother, Rita Shtull, for patience, and for freedom to rely on my own memory and feelings. To my siblings, Kiva, Simcha, and Ora, for encouragement and validation. To my children, Ilanit, Tani, and Leor, for involvement and contribution way beyond the call of duty. To my husband, Steven Leber, for unflagging willingness to read another draft. Because of the loving guidance from family, colleagues, and friends, I am able to share this book with you.

Additional Information About Jack

Rabbi Jacob "Jack" Shtull's parents, Yekutiel Shtull and Blima Schwartz, immigrated to Montreal from what is now eastern Poland, more specifically, from the towns of Tomaszow Lubelski and Zamosc, near the border with Ukraine. Jacob Shtull moved from Montreal to New York City in 1948 and was ordained as a rabbi at the Jewish Theological Seminary of America in 1953. From this institution, he also earned a master's degree in Hebrew literature. Later in life, the seminary awarded him an honorary doctor of divinity degree.

After working in London, Ontario, Rabbi Shtull came to Cleveland in 1957 to serve as rabbi of Mayfield Temple. He was the first English-speaking rabbi of that congregation, which had been founded by German survivors of the Holocaust. In 1970, the congregation merged with Congregation B'nai Israel and was renamed Mayfield Hillcrest Synagogue. It later became known by its Hebrew name, Shaarey Tikvah, which means "Gates of Hope." Rabbi Shtull served as a rabbi for forty-eight years.

Rabbi Shtull taught at Cleveland's College of Jewish Studies, the Jewish Community Center, John Carroll University, and the Menorah Park Center for Senior Living. He initiated classes for Jews by Choice, as well as the annual commemoration in Cleveland of Kristallnacht. A collection of his Kristallnacht commemorations was published in 1983. Rabbi Shtull was also the author of *The Life and Thought of Rabbi Mendel of Kotzk: God's Loyal Rebel.* In his last days, he was collecting notes for a humorous book he had hoped to write about his own hospital experiences.

Rabbi Shtull held national, regional, and local positions, including vice-president of the Rabbinical Assembly of Retired Rabbis, regional director of the United Synagogue, and president of the Cleveland Board of Rabbis. He was present at the United Nations when the new State of Israel first became a member. He marched in Washington to protest the Vietnam War.

Rabbi Shtull wrote numerous articles for the *Cleveland Jewish News*, played clarinet in the Hillcrest Community Band, and was an expert skier, skater, swimmer, tennis player, and dancer. He made pickles and wine and fixed his own car. He took a three-month cruise around the world with his wife, serving as the rabbi on the ship.

Rabbi Shtull was married to Rita (née Estrin, b. 1931). They had four children: Kiva (b. 1953), Simcha (b. 1955), Dina (b. 1957), and Ora (b. 1961). Rabbi Shtull passed away at the age of seventy-six, after being ill for a few years with leukemia. In his memory, the Rabbi Jacob Shtull Memorial Fund and the Rabbi Jacob Shtull Memorial Library have been established at Congregation Shaarey Tikvah in Cleveland.

Made in the USA
San Bernardino, CA
14 August 2018